THE BUDGIE LIKES TO BOOGIE!

Dorset Libraries
Withdrawn Stock

By Brian Moses
Illustrations by Chris White

CABOODLE BOOKS LTD

A Catalogue record for this book is available from the
British Library.

ISBN-13: 978-0-9559711-9-8

Typeset in Century by Paul Wilson

Printed in the UK by CPI Cox & Wyman, Reading

The paper and board used in the paperback by Caboodle
Books Ltd are natural recyclable products made from wood
grown in sustainable forests. The manufacturing processes
conform to the environmental regulations of the country of
origin.

Caboodle Books Ltd
Riversdale, 8 Rivock Avenue, Steeton, BD20 6SA
Tel: 01535 656015

To everyone at
Howard Primary School, Croydon
where I have been welcomed
on many occasions.

Contents

Section 2: Some poems that just feature creatures in one or two lines. Can you spot them?

Section 1

All kinds of poems about all kinds of creatures

The Budgie Likes to Boogie

The budgie likes to boogie,
the budgie likes to rock.
He wakes us every night
when he rocks around the clock.

The budgie likes to jive,
to spin around, to twirl.
His body full of rhythm,
his head is in a whirl.

The budgie boogie-woogies
along the table top.
The budgie disco dances,
the budgie likes to bop.

He's just about the best,
his moves are really neat.
You should see the budgie boogie,
you should see his flying feet!

In front of the dangly mirror,
he plays his air guitar.
The budgie likes to boogie,
the budgie is a STAR!

1

Chocolate Ants

If they started to sell
chocolate covered ants
at the superstore
would you buy them?

If they gave them away
in a tasting test
would you try them?

If they said these are yummy,
and good for you too,
they keep away colds
and protect you from flu.

Would you say
you can give me
a packet or two.

And if you liked them
maybe you'd try...

aniseed fleas
and jelly slugs,
sugar-coated earwigs
or peppermint bugs

a range of tastes
waiting for you,
try 'Eleph - ants'
for a jumbo chew.

But I'd say no way -
I just couldn't,
could you?

Why Kick a Moo Cow?

(There is a vegetarian café in Brighton
called 'Wai Kika Moo Kau')

Why kick a moo cow,
Why kiss a toad,
Why help a chicken
Across the road?

Why bounce a hedgehog,
Why throw a frog,
Why roll a tortoise
Over a log?

Why kick a moo cow,
Why flick a fly,
Why poke a monkey
In the eye?

Why touch a rhino,
Why flip a flea,
Why bring a lizard
Home for tea?

Why kick a moo cow,
Why shake a snake,
Why chuck a duck
Into a lake?

Oh why kick a moo cow?
Why kick a moo cow?
Why kick a moo cow....

Because a moo cow
kicked me, that's why!

The Car Pet Showroom

Bored on long journeys,
tired of the radio,
then visit my showroom -
I do a really nice line
in car pets.

There's a space in your car
that's just right
for the kind of pet
that I have in mind.

A car pet snake
will keep you on your toes,
keep you alert
make sure you don't doze.

Mice are cute
and can live in your boot,
popping in now and then
when you least expect them.

A scorpion for the front seat
when you leave your car.
What a neat way
to deter car thieves.

A lizard for the glove compartment
a family of woodlice
make a nice addition
to an unused ashtray.

The possibilities are endless,
you'll never be friendless
with a car pet.

CAR PETS 1

Walking with my Iguana

(Words in brackets to be repeated by
another voice or voices)

I'm walking (I'm walking)
with my iguana (with my iguana)

I'm walking (I'm walking)
With my iguana (with my iguana)

When the temperature rises
to above eighty-five,
my iguana is looking
like he's coming alive.

So we make it to the beach,
my iguana and me,
then he sits on my shoulder
as we stroll by the sea...

and I'm walking (I'm walking)
with my iguana (with my iguana)

I'm walking (I'm walking)
With my iguana (with my iguana)

Well if anyone sees us
we're a big surprise,
my iguana and me
on our daily exercise,

till somebody phones
the local police
and says I have an alligator
tied to a leash.

when I'm walking (I'm walking)
with my iguana (with my iguana)

I'm walking (I'm walking)
With my iguana (with my iguana)

It's the spines on his back
that make him look grim,
but he just loves to be tickled
under his chin.

And I know that my iguana
is ready for bed
when he puts on his pyjamas
and lays down his sleepy (Yawn) head.

9

And I'm walking (I'm walking)
with my iguana (with my iguana)

still walking (still walking)
With my iguana (with my iguana)

With my iguana ....

with my iguana ....

and my piranha

and my chihuahua

and my chinchilla,

with my gorilla,

my caterpillar.....

and I'm walking......

with my iguana..................

What's Wrong, Doc?

If a leopard's spots are itching
or a warthog gets a wart,
do they hurry to the doctors
for advice?

If giraffes get scared of heights
and skunks no longer smell,
do they hurry to the doc and ask
what's wrong?

If a vulture turns vegetarian
and a turtle sinks like a stone,
if a tiger's stripes go missing
and love birds like to be alone...

If a kangaroo's hop is hopeless
and a hippo is suddenly slim,
if a cheetah loses his speed
and a penguin forgets how to swim...

Do you find them at the surgery,
their faces filled with gloom,
waiting very patiently
in the doctor's waiting room?

11

The Wizard's Cat

When the wizard cast
a spell on his cat,
he was tired, it backfired
and now this cat
is only half the creature
it used to be,
but half a cat
is still company,
still purrs, still warms
the wizard's seat,
still rubs round his legs
and gets under his feet.
But half a cat
is disconcerting
for other cats
when fighting or flirting.
It's doubly feared
this weird half-cat,
this half invisible
acrobat.

The wizard is worried,
he knows that he should
redo the spell
and make it good.
But what would be left
if this spell should fail?
How much of this cat
maybe only a tail.
The wizard too
might be incomplete,
just a wizard's legs
and a wizard's feet.
So best not to meddle
with what's been done,
surely half a cat
is better than none.

The Goldfish's Dream

I'm a nothing special fish
floating about all day.
I open and close my mouth
and don't have a lot to say.
But I have a special dream,
A dream that's really nice.
I dream that I'm an angel fish
swimming in paradise!

The Dog's Favourite Words

The dog has words
she understands.....

Brilliant words like
barking,
ball
and
biscuit.

Irritating words like
cat
and particularly
squirrel.

Adorable words like
dog
and
dinner.

And wondrously, whizzingly
wicked words
like
WALKIES!

The Moth on Our Ceiling

There's a moth on our kitchen ceiling,
he was there all evening,
he was there all night.
If I were a moth with a few days to live
I'd be itchin' to get somewhere else.
It can't be very interesting
watching what happens in our kitchen
or does he find it quite dramatic
when fishcakes burn or a saucepan is dropped.
If I were a moth, I wouldn't be
hanging around on our ceiling,
I'd jump on a Jumbo and head for New York,
or the Caribbean, or the South of France.
Time spent in a deckchair in St. Tropez
has just got to be better
than sticking to our ceiling.

Or maybe it's those occasional moments
that he spends head-butting the light bulb
that make it all worthwhile.
I've got a message for the moth
on our ceiling: Get out, get a life,
go dancing, fall in love, meet a wife,
don't stay up there till you drop.

I wonder what he finds so appealing
about the view from our kitchen ceiling?

My Kung-fu, Kick-boxing Kangaroo

I really haven't a clue what to do
should I sell him for money
or give him to the zoo,
my kung-fu, kick-boxing kangaroo.

He's king of the ring, a middleweight champ.
When he gets really stroppy, you'll hear him stamp,
if you say that he's great he'll light up like a lamp,
my kung-fu, kick-boxing kangaroo.

He's the coolest marsupial I ever knew
he's a real mean fighter, but he's musical too,
plays electric guitar and the didgeridoo,
my kung-fu, kick-boxing kangaroo.

He thinks that lions are no big deal,
he's got muscles like melons and fists of steel,
you won't believe this but he's really real,
my kung-fu, kick-boxing kangaroo.

And I'd avoid him if I were you,
my kung-fu, kick-boxing kangaroo!

A Stick Insect

A stick insect
is not a thick insect,
a macho-built-like-brick insect,
a brawl-and-break-it-up-quick insect,
not a sleek-and-slippery-slick insect
or a hold-your-hand-out-for-a-lick insect.

No way could you say it's a cuddly pet
or a butterfly that hasn't happened yet.

And it won't come running when you call
or chase about after a ball.
And you can't take it out for a walk
or try to teach it how to talk.

It's a hey-come-and-look-at-this-quick insect,
a how-can-you-tell-if-it's-sick insect,
a don't-mistake-me-for-a-stick
       insect...

starfish, you're a star!

I didn't understand
why you were such a star,
starfish...

You don't play football,
you don't drive a car,
you don't sing rock songs
or play guitar....

But you can lose an arm
and then grow a new one,
that's magic....

I gotta hand it to you
starfish,

I'm your fan!

Two Cats

Two cats were yowling
outside of our window last night,
some feline disagreement
that very soon led to a fight.

A bit of an up and downer,
a ding dong, all hell let loose,
fur falling out by the fistful,
no hope of agreeing a truce.

I've met these cats before
when they snatch unwary birds,
then nonchalantly stroll away
despite my barrage of words.

But they soon disappeared this time
when I opened up the door,
threw out a pail of water
and ROARED like a dinosaur!

What if Tyrannosaurus Saw Us?

What if Tyrannosaurus saw us
as we went tiptoeing by?
What if he raised his terrible head
and focussed his bleary eye?

What if Tyrannosaurus saw us,
licked his teeth and thought, 'Here's dinner.'
Could we run and outdistance him
with the speed of an Olympic winner?

We could tell him that we were small fry
and that he'd do better to wait.
Our teacher would be along soon
she'd be meatier meat for the plate.

But what if Tyrannosaurus saw us
and gave a ROAR that shook the trees?
What if our legs refused to move
and we stumbled and fell to our knees?

One thing we know, he wouldn't bore us
with any sort of chit-chat.
He'd open his jaws and gobble us both
in fifteen seconds flat!

But what if Tyrannosaurus saw us,
could we offer him our Smarties,
tell him if he were friendlier
he'd be asked to birthday parties?

Tell him if he stopped bullying
and behaved more sensibly,
then we'd invite him and his family
to call at our house for tea.

The Spider Under
the Stairs

In the darkest corner is a pair of eyes
and I'm sure, for certain, they're growing in size
till they seem to say, now just you dare
take one step further and I'll jump in your hair.

So I reach out quickly and grab the broom
but I hear a movement deep in the gloom,
and I feel like St. George about to do battle
with my broomstick spear and my sister's rattle!

Then something scuttles from its hiding place
and something sticky trails over my face
as the spider spreads its silky threads
winding them round and round my head.

And its coming for me, it's coming now
and I'm shouting, 'MUM, PLEASE COME,' but the row
her hoover makes is all I can hear
and the noise is pounding in my ears.

I'm really naughty Mum says, 'Beware,
or I'll open that cupboard under the stairs
and I'll POP you inside and I won't let you out
no matter how loudly you scream or shout!'

'Oh ssssay you wwwouldn't do that, I say,
my eyes full of fright as I back away.
She smiles and says, 'No, I don't think I would,
but you can't be sure, so you'd better be good!'

The Ssssnake Hotel

An Indian python will welcome you
to the Ssssnake hotel.
As he finds your keys he'll maybe enquire
if you're feeling well.
And he'll say that he hopes
you survive the night,
that you sleep without screaming
and don't die of fright
at the Ssssnake hotel.

There's an anaconda that likes to wander
the corridors at night,
and a boa that will lower itself onto guests
as they search for the light.
And if, by chance, you lie awake
and nearby something hisses,
I warn you now, you're about to be covered
with tiny viper kisses,
at the Ssssnake hotel.

And should you hear a chorus of groans
coming from the room next door,
and the python cracking someone's bones,
please don't go out and explore.
Just ignore all the screams
and the strangled yells
when you spend a weekend
at the Ssssnake hotel.

I'm in Love
with a Slug

I'm in love with a slug
I really think she's neat,
right from the eyes in her antennae
down to the tips of her feet. **

Yes I'm in love with a slug
we meet up every night,
while she's feeding in the lettuces
I watch each tender bite.

I hold her in my hand
as she looks at me with affection.
My heart begins to sing
when faced with such perfection.

If I could shrink to her size
I'd accompany her as she dines,
I'd like to toast her beauty
in a range of dandelion wines.

I know that I'd be the slug
she'd fall in love with too,
and underneath the slippery moon
we'd kiss, the way slugs do!

** Actually slugs only have one 'foot' but
   I needed 'feet' for the rhyme!

Seagulls With Everything

You get seagulls with everything
at St.Ives......

Seagulls with walking sticks,
seagulls with glasses,
seagulls with lipstick
and ones with moustaches.

Seagulls with hats
to cover bald heads,
seagulls with duvets
still lying in bed.

Seagulls with tickets
to travel on trains,
seagulls with telescopes
high up on cranes.

Seagulls with lollies
and ice cream cones,
seagulls with diaries
and mobile phones.

Seagulls in shades
strumming guitars,
seagulls with girlfriends
driving fast cars.

Seagulls with dreams
to fly from St. Ives
and be big movie stars
for the rest of their lives.

I Wish I Could Dine with a Porcupine

I wish I could dine with a porcupine
or take afternoon tea with a whale.
I wish I could race with a cheetah
or visit the house of a snail.

I wish I could chat with a bat
and learn about his habits.
I wish I could dig a deep burrow
and spend the day with rabbits.

I wish I could fly balloons with baboons
or watch jellyfish eating jelly.
I wish I could perfume spray a skunk
so he wouldn't be quite so smelly.

I wish I could learn about a worm
as I slide along on my tummy,
or meet a baby hippo
and his hippotamummy.

I wish I could feast with a wildebeest
or rescue a mule from his load.
I wish I could bake a cake with a snake
or hop down the road with a toad.

I wish I could take all these creatures
for a holiday by the sea,
we'd have our own beach barbecue
and toast marshmallows for tea.

Frogspawn

All those commas
waiting to be born
out of frogspawn.

All those wrigglers
waiting to wriggle.

And all those dots
about to hop.

Watch them quiver,
slide and slither.

A city afloat
or musical notes

that wriggle away
from the bars of a song,

'We won't be long'
they sing.

Questions About Slowworms

Is a slowworm slow
or can he be fast?
On sports days would he
always come last?
Is a slowworm too slow
to meet a mate?
Does he always turn up
late for a date?
I wonder how you tell
a boy from a girl?
When he falls in love
is his head in a whirl?
Does he hear love songs
and feel heartache?
Does he ever wish
he were really a snake?
Does he envy the glow
that a glowworm makes?
Does he have regrets?
Does he make mistakes?
Or is he content
with a warm sunny place?
Is that a smile we can see
on his face?

Robbie The Rooster

Robbie the rooster's in trouble,
one more loud doodle-doo
and his number could be up,
one more yell at high decibels
and he'll be up for the chop.
That's the only way to stop
a rooster crowing
so I'm told.

But Robbie was born to let rip
to give some lip to the other guys
with a screech that would teach them
that he's the boss, top of the heap,
not a rooster to cross,
that when he yells, his proud chest swells,
pumping up the decibels
to more than anyone can stand.

So Robbie the rooster may well be banned
for doing what a rooster does,
and there are no joys in that sort of noise
for anyone living close by,
for anyone woken at 4 a.m.
by his boasting to all the boys.

So when the sun comes over the horizon Robbie
don't let rip with such zip.
Quieten down, maybe mime once or twice
till a time much later in the day.
Then go for it Robbie, give it all you've got,
tell everyone that you're a real big shot,
a rock 'n' rolling rooster that's really hot,
say it loud, say it proud, Robbie Rooster.

A Pet Internet

I feel sorry for our two guinea pigs
cooped up in their hutch together,
staring at each other
staring out at the awful weather.

I feel sorry for cats and dogs
troubled by a niggling doubt
that their owner's won't return from work
and they'll never be let out.

And I really wish that I could supply
a boredom buster for pets,
I'm sure that there'd be a market
for the first pet internet.

Just imagine dogs logging on,
surfing and setting up sites,
or cats in chat rooms complaining
of too many mice free nights.

Rabbits could e-mail forgetful owners,
'Please make sure you feed me',
or a guinea pig needing a girlfriend –
'Hurry up and breed me.'

They'd beat boredom too with games
where cats could hunt virtual mice
and dogs could bury phantom bones
in a canine paradise.

Yes a pet internet would be something to get
how could any pet owner not buy it
with every possible kind of pet
all desperate to try it.

Peculiar Pets

I've got a dog that whistles
and a stick insect that snores.
I've got a rabbit that would rather
watch TV than be out-of-doors.

I've got gerbils that perform
several of Shakespeare's plays.
I've got a tortoise that drinks
frothy coffee in street cafés.

I've got a fish that tells fortunes
and guinea pigs that rap.
I've got cats that play in a rock band
and a budgie that dances tap.

I've got a rat that looks quite hip
in the latest designer suit,
and a hamster that writes love letters
to a rather attractive newt.

Yes, I've got a dog that whistles
and a stick insect that snores.
These are my peculiar pets
now tell me about some of yours!

A Protest About Cabbage

Our guinea pigs are making
a protest about cabbage.

Each evening we feed them cabbage
but the cabbage stays uneaten.

They know they can outsmart us,
they have stated their campaign.

Okay, when they put us in our run,
eat as much grass as you can stomach,
fill up with enough to last,
then when they throw in the cabbage,
sit tight, we're on hunger strike.

Well actually they don't really say it like that,
they use guinea pig speak :

Squeak, squeak, squeak, squeak grass
squeak, squeak, squeak, squeak lovely.
Squeak, squeak, squeak, squeak cabbage
squeak, squeak, squeak, squeak YUK!

Pretty soon we'll stop giving them cabbage
and they know it.

Lettuce and carrot are both OK
but they swoon at the thought of grass.
Grass to a guinea pig is
angel delight,
strawberries and cream,
Black Forest gateaux,
and Death by Chocolate.

But when I tried it – BIG DISAPPOINTMENT!

I don't know what they see in grass
but I know what they mean about cabbage!

Next Door's Cat

Next door's cat lost
a couple of lives last night.
Serve him right for
hanging round our pond,
seeking some fresh fish dish
to supplement his diet.

So out I crept behind the shed,
then slid on my belly, crocodile style,
while my target eyeballed the pond.

And I let him have just one more moment
of peace and contemplation,
before I let him have it ......

I LEAPT and I ROARED
I HOLLERED and I YELLED
I WARDANCED and I SCREAMED,
I YAHOOED and I SCREEEEEECHED...

And I swear I saw a miracle
out there in our back garden,
when next door's cat walked on water
to escape the wrath of a demon.

Old Black Dog

Did you ever see such an old black dog?

A laze about in the warm French sun dog.
A pat me if you like
  but you won't make me get up and run dog.
A once upon a time I'd play
  with a ball in the park dog.
A now I'm too tired and I can't be bothered to bark dog.

A cats don't worry me like they used to do dog,
  but if one of them invades my space
    I'll still show them a thing or two dog.
A don't expect me to hear you when you call dog,
a leave me to dream, and let me sprawl dog.

A scratch my tummy,
  look for me
where it's sunny

  dog.

45

Fleas !

Fleas have been seen in this school,
Fleas have been seen in this house,
Fleas that would frighten elephants,
Fleas the size of a mouse.
Fleas with fangs like vampires,
Fleas with hungry smiles.
Fleas with enormous jaws
And teeth like crocodiles.

Fleas have been seen body-building,
Fleas have been seen at the gym,
Fleas have been lifting weights
And keeping themselves in trim.
Fleas have been learning karate,
Ju-jitsu and kung-fu.
Fleas are now fit for a fight

And they're coming after YOU ....!

Never Seen

Never seen a hyena with a vacuum cleaner,
never seen a goat in a boat.
Never seen a pike on a motorbike
but I've seen an anaconda in a Honda.

Never seen a fish in a satellite dish,
never seen a whale in the Royal Mail.
Never seen a llama unpeel a banana
but I've seen an anaconda in a Honda.

Never seen a tadpole do a forward roll,
never seen a frog weightlifting a log.
Never seen a poodle cooking noodles
but I've seen an anaconda in a Honda.

Never seen a panda in an armoured tank,
never seen a tortoise at a taxi rank.
Never seen a tiger rob a national bank
but I've seen an anaconda in a Honda.

And I've watched him wander and weave

all over the road.

My Sister Said

My sister said,
'If you do that to me again,
   I'll put ....

Slugs in your shoes,
spiders in your vest,
earwigs in your ear
and caterpillars in your cornflakes.

   I'll put....
beetles between your sheets,
squirmy worms in your hair,
centipedes in your lunchbox
and grasshoppers, (real whoppers) in your slippers.

   I'll put....
ants in your knickers,
woodlice under your pillow,
snails in your school bag
and nits in your nightwear.'

'I'll really make you scream,' she said,
'You'll yell and shake and shiver......'

And I know that she will,
and I promise I won't .... NOT EVER!

Monty

(For the Wallace Family)

Monty doesn't move much anymore,
his world reduced to rooms downstairs,
a favourite mat, can't climb on chairs,
no threat to cats anymore.

Monty doesn't see much anymore,
his vision, once sharp, now plays tricks,
can't see where to look if someone throws sticks,
no way he can play anymore.

Monty doesn't hear much anymore,
his bark won't shake the house from sleep,
when burglars broke in, not a peep,
nothing disturbs anymore.

But Monty dreams, deep sweet dreams,
of a dog that swims and rolls and chases,
long wet tongue licking hands and faces
and nothing hurts anymore.

Mind That Dog!

Just watch it or Rufus will get you,
he'll sort you out in a flash,
he'll make you move so fast
you'll win a medal in the half mile dash.

Just watch it or Rufus will get you,
he's nabbed many children before,
he'll knock you down and shove you around
then leave you flat on the floor.

Rufus likes to show who's boss
but worse, far worse than this,
is when Rufus pins you down on the ground
and gives you a slobbery kiss!

Lovesick Snail

A giant African land snail
has fallen in love with our teacher,
his eyes are out on stalks, you can tell
he's besotted, this lovelorn creature.
If you look closely you'll see him
blowing kisses across the room,
this giant African snail with a crush
and no hope of lifting his gloom.
And we really couldn't blame him,
our teacher is awfully nice.
We know for a fact that she's also adored
by stick insects, gerbils and mice.

Lizards don't eat flies

There's an odd little fact
about lizards
that not many people know -
they can't stand flies
and they'd rather eat fries.
So they wait around at
takeaways,
hoping there might be
throwaways
left in the bag
when somebody bins it.

Yes, lizards hate flies
and would rather eat fries
anyday

(especially with vinegar!)

Jellyfish

Jellyfish,
jellyfish,
floats along and slaps you on the belly
fish.

Just when you thought you'd go for a swim,
just when thought it was safe to go in.

Jellyfish,
jellyfish,
saw one in a programme on the telly
fish.

Thinking about it kept me awake,
I just don't think that I can take

jellyfish,
jellyfish,
trod on one at Margate
with Aunt Nelly
fish.

If you see one in the sea then give me a shout,
catch it in a bucket but keep your fingers out.

Jellyfish,
jellyfish,
odd and funny-looking umbrelly
fish,
slimy old seaside smelly
fish,

jellyfish,
jellyfish,
jellyfish,
jellyfish.

Hippopotamus Dancing

In the hippo house
at the city zoo,
hippos are moving
to the boogaloo,
big hippos shuffle,
little hippos trot,
everyone giving it
all they've got...

Hip-hippo, hippopotamus dancing,
hip-hippo, hippopotamus dancing,

Every hippo
keeping fit,
fighting the flab
doing their bit,
weight training one week,
aerobics another,
tiny hippopotami
move with their mothers...

Hip-hippo, hippopotamus dancing,
hip-hippo, hippopotamus dancing.

Hippos in tutus,
hippos in vests,
baby hippos
doing their best
to keep clear of dad
as he stumbles around,
causing commotion,
shaking the ground...

Hip-hippo, hippopotamus dancing,
hip-hippo, hippopotamus dancing.

There's a Hamster in the Fast Lane

The speed cameras are flashing
but they can't indentify
a hamster in the fast lane
as he roly-polys by.

He doesn't show a number
and shades obscure his eyes.
Police reports all tell of some
boy racer in disguise.

For everyone who sees him
he's the cause of mirth and mayhem.
He's passing big fat four wheel drives
by rolling underneath them.

No more tickles on the tummy,
no more crummy little cage.
One hundred miles an hour at least,
fuelled by hamster rage.

He's passing open tops,
he's passing executive cars.
His energy is endless,
no sleep till Zanzibar!

He's belting down the bypass
like a speed king on a track,
unsure of where he's going
but he knows he won't be back!

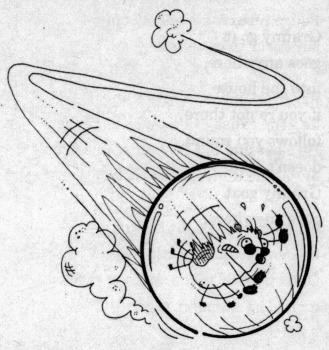

Granny Goat

Eat anything
will granny goat,
handkerchiefs,
the sleeve of your coat,
sandwiches,
a ten pound note.
Eat anything
will granny goat.

Granny goat
goes anywhere,
into the house
if you're not there,
follows you round,
doesn't care.
Granny goat
goes anywhere.

Granny goat
won't stay
tied up
throughout the day,
chews the rope,
wants to play.
Granny goat
won't stay

anywhere you
want her to,
she'd rather be
with you!

Frog Street

(Frog Street is a small village in Essex)

Do they look at the world
through big bulgy eyes
in Frog Street?

Do they eat their burgers
with flies not fries
in Frog Street?

Do they sleep like a log
or under a log?
Are they looking out
for princesses to snog?

Do they have slimy bodies
and small webbed feet?
Tell me, who on earth lives
in Frog Street?

1 Dare You

I dare you to find a dragon
and climb on its scaly back.
I dare you to enter its cave
and fill up your treasure sack.

I dare you to touch a dragon's tooth,
I dare you to tickle its chin.
I dare you to dodge the flames
that flicker from the fire within.

I dare you to ask it to dance
and to make sure you tread on its toes.
I dare you to call it dragon breath
and walk away holding your nose.

I dare you...

Fox

We've never seen a hare in Hare Way,
cats and dogs of course, the occasional horse,
but last night we saw a fox.
In the time it took to do a double take,
he'd looked at us and looked away,
he was keen to be about his business,
we were no worry to him.

In the newly darkened evening
we were pleased we'd seen
a fox with no worries
out for a stroll,
pleased our paths had crossed,
that we'd spent those briefest of seconds
watching him, watching us, watching him.

FISHY!

At the Sea Life Centre
there were plenty of fish,
floating and gliding or
chasing about,
but although we saw
fish tails and fish scales,
teeth and mouths,
whiskers and fins,
we didn't see any
fishfingers!

Flash Fish

(In the Dingle Aquarium, Ireland)

For a fish, she's a Mercedes,
a fish that knows she's flash,
a fish that knows she's turning heads
when she makes the occasional dash

slipping from rock to hidey-hole
at strike of lightning speed
in an effort to burn off calories
and hoping to succeed

in winning admiration
for her contours and her poise,
she's a fish that knows she's flash
and so do all the boys.

You can see them looking on,
you can see how much they wish
that they meant something special
to this fish that's such a dish.

But she's far too hoity-toity
and scares them all away.
'Come back when you grow up,'
you can almost hear her say.

She's a dolphin wannabe herself,
unhappy with her lot,
she knows she really should be
something that she's not,

a model perhaps, or a film star
with millions in the bank,
not a fish that just exists
inside this grotty tank.

She hopes that maybe one day
some film director might see
the talent that she has
and what a catch she'd be.

There must be something better,
there's got to be, she's sure.
Someone once found Nemo
so surely they'll find her!

Dressed Crabs

What do crabs wear when they're dressed,
do we see them in suits and ties,
do the ladies all wear ballgowns
and carefully make up their eyes?

Do they stand in front of a mirror
and reckon they look pretty neat
do they wear stiletto heels
with toes that pinch their feet?

And when they're dressed to kill
where do you think they go?
Are they off to a high class party
or a seat at a West End show?

No, crabs have only one destination
a cold hard fishmonger's slab,
that's the place you need to look
to spot the well dressed crab.

Wish

Clasp in your hand
the single black feather
left in your garden
as a gift from a crow

Whisper the words
that you learnt from the wind,

Find dragonfly spit
and a snake's shed skin.

Find a flower's heartbeat
and the moon's lost silver

Now gather them together
with the crow's black feather...

and WISH.......

A Spider the Size of Godzilla

A spider the size of Godzilla
lay in wait at the bend in the stairs,
and no one dared to pass it alone
we all had to sneak by in pairs.

Already the spider had hollowed out
a hidey hole in the wall
and was patiently waiting to pounce
should anyone stumble and fall.

It had laser piercing eyes
and legs as thick as rope,
a brush and dustpan was useless
it was slippery as soap.

And I think we would all have preferred
a lion or a mountain gorilla,
because no one felt like tackling
a spider the size of Godzilla.

We hadn't a big enough jam-jar
to trap this unwelcome guest,
and no one came to our aid
even though we S.O.S-ed.

But the spider must have decided
the time was right for retreat.....
It karate kicked a hole in our wall
and disappeared down the street.

Danielle's Dragon

Danielle was sure
she'd seen dragon's breath
out beyond the headland.

'There's a cave in the next bay,' she said.
'That's where she'll have her lair.'

We said we'd go and look
but I knew before we set out
we'd be lucky.

Just like our trip to the rainbow's end
or the afternoon we'd dug in the yard
thinking we'd reach Australia.

But Danielle was able to make us believe
we'd seen what she'd seen
and that what she said was gospel,
cross-your-heart talk.

So we trudged where the tide was out,
picking up this and that on the way,
till we rounded the headland and there
in the bay was some old tramp
with a bonfire, and smoke curling into the sky.

He was boiling something yuk in a can
and he called, 'Come on ladies,
there's plenty for all!'

But we took one look at
his gap-toothed grin, and his baked-bean cans
with the liquid in,
and we turned and ran as fast as we could

as if dragon's breath was tagging our heels.

We couldn't have been more scared
if Danielle's dragon had really been real!

Crossing the Border

Our cat is a sweetie, how could we leave her
when we're moving home from Brussels to Geneva,
and our rabbit too, he just had to come,
and our two guinea pigs, a daughter and her mum...

So we're crossing the border with an illegal rabbit,
two guinea pigs and a cat,
and we don't make a habit of breaking the law
but it really has come to that.
And we hope no one spots the heap of coats
when they move in the back of our car
and we hope the border patrols won't notice
the smell, now we've travelled this far.
If they catch a glimpse of a twitching nose
then this journey of ours will have failed.
If the cat should yowl we'll be caught,
if the guinea pigs squeal we'll be jailed.
So stay calm, keep quiet, say nothing
or there won't be a welcome mat
when we're crossing the border with an illegal rabbit,
two guinea pigs and a cat.

The Aquarium

The aquarium
was disappointing:

The dogfish
didn't bark,
the jellyfish
didn't wobble.

The sea mouse
didn't squeak,
the starfish
didn't shine.

The hermit crabs
were crabby,
the clams
clammed up,
and the plaice
stayed in one place.

But when the swordfish
attacked us,
and the sharks invited us
to be their lunch...

we rode away fast...
on a sea horse!

It's a Short Hop
to a Habitat Swap

You've heard about changing rooms,
well, why can't animals do it too?
Dolphin swap with eagle,
penguin with kangaroo.

Polar bear offers snow hole,
gorilla quits jungle den,
camel gives up the desert
for a home in a Scottish glen.

Termites leave their mounds
for a coral reef under the sea.
A mole grown tired of a hole
is fixing a nest in a tree.

Badger offers his burrow
to a lobster and a crab,
but who will swap places
with a slug sleeping under a slab,

Or a spider who offers a web
but doesn't say when he's leaving?
Well, it could turn out to be true
but it all takes some believing.

Animals changing habitats -
it might catch on at the zoo,
every year, when spring comes round,
old homes being swapped for new.

The Cat that Bites Back

(For Judith)

Sure, you rescued me
when I was a scruff,
so I ought to be grateful
and not play rough,

And you feed me tuna,
the finest brands,
but I still can't help it
if I nip your hands,

'cause I'm the cat,
the cat that bites back.

I'm more than feline,
I'm felion,
tough as cowhide,
strong as iron.

I call the shots,
I'm the top of the heap,
when I want something
humans leap...

'cause I'm the cat,
the cat that bites back.

I'm the cat that bites
the hands that feed me
but I'm not bothered,
I know you need me.

Your angry looks
are mixed with pity
but I'll never be
your cuddly kitty...

'cause I'm the cat,
the cat that bites back.

I'm the cat,
the cat that bites back...

PURRRRROAR !

Bigfoot

Our house is full of Bigfoot
or should that be Bigfeet?
We watched them from our window
as they stumbled down the street.

They knocked upon our door
and asked to come inside.
'Don't leave us here,' they pleaded,
'We need a place to hide.'

Now there's Bigfeet in the kitchen
and Biggerfeet in the hall.
On a patch of grass in our garden,
Bigfeet are playing football.

There's Bigfeet in our garage
and Bigfeet in the shed,
while underneath the duvet,
Bigfeet sleep in my bed.

Bigfeet lounge in the lounge
all watching our TV.
There's nowhere much to sit
since they've broken our settee.

Some Bigfoot put his foot
right through our bedroom ceiling.
The darkness in our loft, he said,
was really quite appealing.

The airing cupboard Bigfoot
keeps our water hot.
'No problem at all,' he says,
'I like this job a lot.'

They make an awful racket
up and down our stairs,
they queue to use the bathroom
and block the sink with hairs.

At night they growl and snore,
loud as a thunderstorm,
but all these fur coats everywhere
keep us cosy and warm!

At the Zoo

If you want to get married at London Zoo
this is what we can offer you...

A four metre long reticulated snake
gift-wrapped round your wedding cake.
A choir of hyenas singing loud,
a congregation of apes from rent-a-crowd.
Two charming chimps that will bridesmaid you
and if you need a witness use a kangaroo
at the zoo, at the zoo, at the zoo.

The waiters look great in their penguin suits,
the monkeys will serve you selected fruits.
The alligators are simply delighted,
even ocelots get quite excited.
The Vietnamese pot-bellied pigs
will take to their toes and dance wedding jigs
at the zoo, at the zoo, at the zoo.

The lions look forward to welcoming you
to your wedding breakfast here at the zoo,
and any leftovers they'd be please to chew
at the zoo, at the zoo, at the zoo.

Yes, we look forward to marrying you
at the zoo, at the zoo, at the zoo.

At the Vets

When we took our dog to the vets
we sat and waited with all kinds of pets.

There were hamsters with headaches
and fish with the flu,
there were rats and bats
and a lame kangaroo.

There were porcupines
with spines that were bent
and a poodle that must have been
sprinkled with scent.

There were dogs that were feeling
terribly grumpy
and monkeys with mumps looking
awfully lumpy.

There were rabbits with rashes
and foxes with fleas,
there were thin mice in need of
a large wedge of cheese.

There were cats complaining
of painful sore throats,
there were gerbils and geese
and two travel sick goats.

There were two chimpanzees
who both had toothache,
and the thought of the vet made everyone

Shake!

The Anaconda Wanderers

The Anaconda Wanderers
are a wonderful football team.
They strike with such precision,
they're every manager's dream.

They're snaking up the league,
dirty foulers everyone,
winding themselves round legs
so the other team can't run.

No one wants to play them,
they are big and slinky and mean.
They threaten to damage the ref
if he favours the opposite team.

Don't hiss or boo or jeer them,
you'd be making foolish mistakes,
you may suddenly find yourself visited
by a gang of angry snakes.

They're the Anaconda Wanderers,
winning every competition,
slippery in midfield
tying up the opposition,

keeping them all in knots,
knowing they will defeat them.
And if by chance they shouldn't
they'll just squeeze them to death....
                and then eat them!

An Unlikely Alphabet of Animals in Even Unlikelier Places

Aylesbury is the area for aardvarks
and Bellingham is brimming with bees.
In Carlisle you'll come across caterpillars
and in Dover you'll see donkeys.
In Egham, elephants are everywhere
While in Frome all you'll find are frogs.
Grimsby is great for goats
and Hastings is home to hot dogs!
In the Isle of Islay I spied iguanas
and in Jarrow I juggled with jellyfish
In Kirklees I was kind to koalas
but llamas in London were loutish.
Meercats have moved into Margate
and Newbury is well known for newts.
Orang Utangs are oafish in Oxford
and penguins in Penge wear playsuits.
Quetzels are quiet in Queenborough
but rhinos are roaring in Rochdale.
Squirrels surf in the seas off St. Ives
while turtles in Taunton tell tales.

Umbrella birds unwind in Ullapool
while vipers are venomous in Villaze.
Wildebeests wait in Warrington
for X ray fish Xeroxing x rays.
Yaks yawn in Yarmouth and long for their beds
and all you get from zebras in Zennor are zzzzs.

(Note – all these places do exist. Villaze is on
Guernsey but there are no places in the UK
beginning with 'X' according to my atlas!)

A Sea Creature Ate Our Teacher

Our teacher said that it's always good
to have an inquisitive mind,
then he told us, 'Go check the rock pools,
let's see what the tide's left behind.'

The muscles on his arms were bulging
as he pushed rocks out of the way,
'Identify what you see,' he called,
'Note it down in your book straightaway.'

It was just as he spoke when we smelt it
a stench, like something rotten,
a wobbling mass of wet black skin
like something time had forgotten.

In front of us snaking up from the pool
was a hideous slime-soaked creature
with a huge black hole of a mouth
that vacuumed up our teacher.

I didn't actually see him go,
I was looking away at the time,
but I saw two legs sticking out
and trainers covered in slime.

But our teacher must have given this creature
such chronic indigestion.
It found out soon that to try and digest him
was simply out of the question.

It gave an almighty lunge of its neck
and spat our teacher out.
He was spread with the most revolting goo
and staggering about.

None of us moved to help him
as he wiped the gunge from his head.
We looked at each other and smirked,
'That'll teach him a lesson,' we said!

DJ Croc

Hi
I'm DJ Croc
I'm one big rapper,
I'm King of the Nile
Call me Super Snapper.

You should see me shimmy
you should see me smile
as I strut my stuff
on the banks of the Nile.

I'm one hot ticket
I can really move,
doesn't take much
to get me in the groove.

Just a hip and a hop
and I'm ready to bop,
reelin' and a rockin'
till I just can't stop.

Yes I'm DJ Croc
I'm one big rapper,
I'm King of the Nile
Call me Super Snapper.

Don't call me Big Mouth
to my face
or I might just knock you
about the place.

But I'd never get
on MTV
if I forget my manners
and have you for tea.

So I'm rapping away
and don't get me wrong,
but I love to sample
my favourite song.

Never smile at me 'cause I'm a crocodile,
Never tip your hat ....
(You know the rest!!!!!)

Yes I'm DJ Croc
I'm one big rapper,
I'm King of the Nile
Call me Super Snapper.

The Alligator Waiter

Don't give any lip
to an alligator waiter.
Don't growl or howl
when he's on the prowl.
Don't mock him or knock him
or say that he's shocking.
He really isn't the sort to say:
'Enjoy your meals,'
or, 'Have a nice day!'
And if you should joke
or poke fun at his snout
you'll need to give
your Mum a shout.
And make sure you tip
or he'll catch you later.
Don't give any lip
to an alligator waiter.

Section 2:

Some poems that just feature creatures in one or two lines.

Can you spot them?

My Little Sister

My little sister
doesn't kick, or thump, or scratch, or slog you,
my little sister
just wants to snog you....

And if you're not quick to escape
she'll nab you,
she'll take you by surprise
and grab you....

And it isn't a peck on the neck
or the briefest brush of the lips,

She's an artist who likes
to paint your face

with a sliding kiss
that seems like a snail
has left its trail on your cheek!

Wriggle Room

When it's assembly time
and you're sitting in line,
what do you need,
you need wriggle room.

When it's a bit of strain
on a railway train,
what do you need,
you need wriggle room.

When you're tucked up in bed
with your favourite ted,
what do you need,
you need wriggle room.

When you're travelling far
in the back of a car,
what do you need,
you need wriggle room.

All the penguins in the zoo
need wriggle room.
A baby kangaroo
needs wriggle room.

All the angels in Heaven
need wriggle room.
Man U first eleven
need wriggle room.

All the motorway cars
need wriggle room.
The moon and the stars
need wriggle room.

Frogs on a log
need wriggle room.
Fleas on a dog
need wriggle room.

Every boy & every girl
needs wriggle room.
In an overcrowded world
what do we need?

WRIGGLE ROOM!

Wriggle room,
wriggle room,
wriggle room,
wriggle room.

What do we need?
We need
wriggle room!

Wriggle!

Wriggle!

Don't Be Such a Fusspot

Don't be such a fusspot,
an always-in-a-rushpot.

Don't be such a weepypot,
a sneak-to-mum-and-be-creepypot.

Don't be such a muddlepot,
a double-dose-of-troublepot.

Don't be such a wigglepot,
a sit-on-your-seat-don't-squigglepot.

Don't be such a muckypot,
a pick-up-slugs-and-be-yuckypot.

Don't be such a sleepypot,
a beneath-the-bedclothes-peepypot.

Don't be such a fiddlepot,
a mess-about-and-meddlepot.

Don't be such a bossypot,
a saucypot, a gigglepot,
don't be such a lazypot,
a nigglepot, a slackpot.

And don't call me a crackpot....
Who do you think you are?

Wait in the Car

When Mum says, 'Wait in the car,
I'll only be gone a minute,'
she's always longer.
We read or play games
and then start to worry.
Perhaps she's run away for good,
she always said she would
if we didn't behave.
Perhaps she's been kidnapped
by bank robbers and bundled into
their getaway car.
Perhaps she's been run over
by a steamroller,
or hypnotised by a magician,
or savaged by a pack
of hungry Pekingese.
Perhaps she's picked a fight
with a Sumo wrestler!

And when she does come back
it's always 'Sorry kids,
but I met an old friend
and we had such a lot to talk about,'
or, 'I just popped into that shop
as they had a sale on....'
And we hide our yawns
and think how boring
our Mum is.

How Can I!

How can I wind up my brother
when I haven't got the key?

How can I turn on my charm
when I can't even find the switch?

How can I snap at my mother
when I'm not a crocodile?

How can I stir up my sister
when I'm not even holding a spoon?

How can I pick up my feet
and not fall to the ground on my knees?

How can I stretch my legs
when they're long enough already?

Parents! – They ask the impossible!

Meeting Mum's Old Boyfriend

'Meet the man who was nearly your dad,' mum said,
'If he hadn't have gone away.'
'What's the matter, cat got your tongue?'
But I just didn't know what to say.

It's weird to find that someone else's dad
might have been mine, if he'd stayed,
and weirder still to meet up with him,
I must have looked really dismayed.

He's got more money than we have,
he looks younger, less worn out.
He's got a big house in the country
and a smart flash car, no doubt.

But I bet he couldn't make me laugh
like my dad does when I'm sad.
And I bet he wouldn't know the right words
to calm me down when I'm mad.

And I bet he couldn't cuddle like my dad can
or tickle me in all the right places.
or read aloud like my dad does
or pull such funny faces.

I'm glad mum married the dad that I have,
and I'm sure that my mum really knew
that the man before dad wasn't right for her,
and my dad says he told her that too!

Ellie's Smelly Wellies

(These days you can actually buy
wellington boots that smell of
strawberries!)

Everyone wanted to smell
Ellie's smelly wellies.

Rose said they smelt of roses.

Lily said definitely lilies.

India caught a whiff
of curry.

Rosemary said rosemary,
with maybe some parsley and thyme.

Lavender said lavender.

Primrose caught the scent of spring
and Blossom did too.

Only Hermione, who didn't like Ellie,
said that Ellie's wellies
smelt of cow poo!

But Ellie didn't care.

When she squeezed her toes
deep into her wellies
she smelt

cut grass
Spanish oranges,
sea breezes,
strawberry teas

and only the very slightest trace

of cowpat!

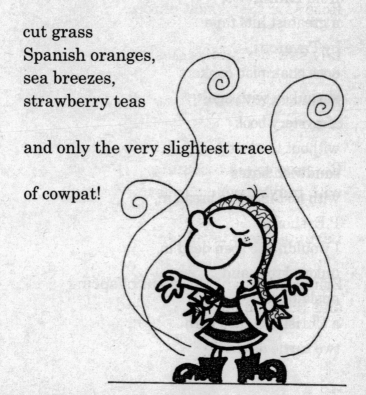

Lost Property Box

In our lost property box
there are socks with holes in
and shoes minus laces,
stand-up figures
without any bases,
a faded T-shirt
from Lanzarotte,
a greatest hits tape
by Pavarotti,
once champion conkers
shrunken with age,
a mystery book
without the last page,
sandwich boxes
with last month's bread in,
P.E. shorts,
I wouldn't be seen dead in,
unloved toys and
mislaid gloves,
a Christmas card with
two turtle doves,

red underpants
decidedly manky,
a barely used
lace-edged hanky,
a love letter
from David Pratt
to his girlfriend Sally,
what about that!
And right at the bottom,
what I'm looking for,
the sports shirt I borrowed
from the boy next door...

Perhaps he won't bash me
now I've found it!

JCB

I'm in love with a JCB,
it's huge, it's greedy and it eats messily,
gulping up great gobfuls of food
then spitting it out, mum calls that rude!

I watch it all day as it lumbers about
while the men stand round it and signal or shout:
'More over here Jack, get stuck in...'
and the engine cranks up a dreadful din.

The head swings round to look at me
like some dinosaur from pre-history.
Its jaws snap shut like a terrible trap
but the man in the cab never gets in a flap,

he sits there calmly turning the wheel,
throwing levers, how does it feel
to be in control of such a beast
as each day it scoffs its enormous feast?

Oh I'm in love with a JCB,
but I don't think that it's in love with me!
It turns its head and looks my way,
It opens its mouth as if to say:

114

'Better scoot before I grab you,
better scram before I nab you...'
I don't like the look that it's giving me,
I'm not in love with a JCB
        after all!

Spring in the City

Spring has come to the city,
to the streets and the railway line.
Winter is packing its bags,
the sun has begun to shine

The cherry tree in our garden
wears a wedding dress of white.
Geese are in flight once more
and days are warm with delight.

There are plenty of baby lambs
to feed at the city farm,
and a single primrose shows its head
at the dump like a lucky charm.

A heron is raising its young
at the flooded gravel pits,
and the nest box on out garden wall
is a home for baby tits.

Wrens are finding new homes
in an untidy, overgrown hedge.
Pigeons keep to their buildings
and jostle for space on a ledge.

Spring has come to the city,
there's a lightness in everyone's tread.
Office workers have shed their coats,
there's a promise of summer ahead.

Christmas Eve

I'm trying to sleep on Christmas Eve
but I really can't settle down,
and I don't want to lie
with wide open eyes
till the morning comes around.

I hear Mum and Dad downstairs,
doing their best to keep quiet,
and although I'm in bed
with my favourite ted,
in my head there's a terrible riot.

I'm thinking of Christmas morning
and all the presents I'll find,
but what if I've missed
something good off my list,
it keeps going round in my mind.

Mum has been baking all day
making rolls, mince pies and cake,
and I know quite well
it's this heavenly smell
that's keeping me wide awake.

Perhaps I'll slip down for some water
though I ought to stay in my room,
but maybe I'll risk
a slap with the whisk
for a lick of Mum's mixing spoon.

If I had just one mince pie
then I know it would be alright,
fast asleep,
not another peep,
my eye shut tightly all night.

Now Dad says Father Christmas
won't leave any presents for me,
Make no mistake,
if you're still awake
he'll pass you by, you'll see!

But I've tried and I've tried and I've tried
and I keep rolling round in my bed,
I still can't sleep,
and I'm fed up with sheep
so I'm counting reindeer instead!

Yell Baby, Yell!

It was coming through loud and clear,
from the baby's room right down to my ear,
a glorious noise, a tremendous din,
like someone scraping a violin.

yow-ow-ow-ow-ow-ow-ow-ow-ow!!

I was really amazed, I just didn't dream
that something so small could holler and scream
like Pavarotti on a chewed up tape
when she opens her mouth and lets it escape.

yow-ow-ow-ow-ow-ow-ow-ow-ow!!

I ran to the garden, I wanted to hide
but I even heard Radio Baby outside,
and I had to admit it, I was really impressed,
on any noisemeter she's be the best

yow-ow-ow-ow-ow-ow-ow-ow-ow!!

Now if anyone calls they don't stay very long,
even our cat has packed up and gone,
The neighbours can't sleep, they look dreadfully pale
and I hear that they're putting their house up for
sale.

yow-ow-ow-ow-ow-ow-ow-ow-ow!!

Hide and Seek

Hide and seek
all down the street,
behind parked cars,
look out for their feet.
Inside a dustbin
ugh, you stink!
Stupid place to hide,
I just didn't think.
Crouch down behind walls
in someone's front yard –
my knees are hurting,
this concrete's hard.
I know that they'll find me,
they always do,
I wish I could find
somewhere good, like you.
But something happens
to give me away,
a dog starts barking
or I hear someone say:

'Hey you by the fence,
get away from there.'
So I give myself up,
it just isn't fair.
I dream that I'll find
somewhere perfect one day
and I'll hide there forever
till they all go away.

The Magic Kingdom

This is the Magic Kingdom
this is where the magic begins.

And you hug it and hold it
in the shape of a bear.
And you wear the magic
in a wizard's hat.
And you ride with the magic
in breathtaking flights.
And you're scared by the magic
when it creeps up behind you.
And you move with the magic
till your feet ache from dancing.

And at night the magic shifts,
changes, rearranges itself
into a lullaby
and rocks you to sleep.

And when it's time to leave
you think that you'll lose it,
you think that you'll leave
all the magic behind
but hey presto,
it travels with you.
It hides in your pocket,
it sneaks into your bag,
it touches your home, your family,
and it brightens up the dull
and the ordinary days....

until the next time it pulls you back
to the Magic Kingdom.

Dreamer

I dreamt I was an ocean
and no one polluted me.

I dreamt I was a whale
and no hunters chased after me.

I dreamt I was the air
and nothing blackened me.

I dreamt I was a stream
and nobody poisoned me.

I dreamt I was an elephant
and nobody stole my ivory.

I dreamt I was a rain forest
and no one cut down my trees.

I dreamt I painted a smile
on the face of the Earth
for all to see.

Brian Moses writes poetry and picture books for children and resource books for teachers.

For the past 21 years he has toured his poetry and percussion show around schools, libraries and theatres throughout the United Kingdom and abroad.

He has published over 180 books and his poems are regularly featured on CBBC and on BBC radio.

You can read an interview with Brian at **www.poetryzone.co.uk**

You can listen to Brian's poetry and percussion at **www.poetryarchive.org**

Other books by Brian Moses:

- Behind the Staffroom Door: The Very Best of Brian Moses (Macmillan)

- Greetings Earthlings: Space poems (with James Carter) (Macmillan)

- Taking Out the Tigers - poems by Brian Moses (Macmillan)

- The Snake Hotel - picture book (Macmillan)

- Trouble at the Dinosaur Café (Puffin Picture Book)

- Beetle in the Bathroom (Puffin picture book)

- The Secret Lives of Teachers - (Macmillan anthology)

- There's a Hamster in the Fast Lane - Pet Poems (Macmillan anthology)

- Aliens Stole My Underpants (Macmillan anthology)

- Walking With My Iguana (Hodder anthology)